Wild Life of Snakes™

COPPERHEADS

HEATHER FELDMAN

The Rosen Publishing Group's
PowerKids Press™

For Pam and Kaare Weber, two very special friends

Published in 2004 by The Rosen Publishing Group, Inc.
29 East 21st Street, New York, NY 10010

First Edition

Editor: Kathy Kuhtz Campbell
Book Design: Mike Donnellan, Michael de Guzman

Photo Credits: Cover, p. 19 © Peter May; back cover, p. 8 © David A. Northcott/CORBIS; pp. 4, 12 (inset), 15, 15 (inset), 20 © Joe McDonald/CORBIS; p. 7 © Clive Druett/CORBIS; p. 11 © Dominique Braud/Animals Animals; p. 12 © Carmela Leszcznski/Animals Animals; p. 16 © Color-Pic/Animals Animals.

Feldman, Heather.
Copperheads / Heather Feldman.—1st ed.
     v. cm.— (The Really wild life of snakes)
Includes bibliographical references (p.   ).
Contents: Copper-colored snakes—Cold-blooded copperheads—Copperhead homes—A snake with catlike eyes—Pit vipers—Copperhead venom—Mating—Baby copperheads—Molting—Copperheads and people.
  ISBN 0-8239-6721-2 (lib. bdg.)
1. Copperhead—Juvenile literature. [1. Copperhead. 2. Snakes.] I. Title. II. Series.
  QL666.O69 F448 2004
  597.96'3—dc21
                                                                    2002012665

Manufactured in the United States of America

CONTENTS

COPPER-COLORED SNAKES

Copperheads are shy, poisonous snakes. The heads of most of these snakes are the color of a new penny. This reddish brown color, called copper, gives the snake its name. The color of each snake's body depends on where the snake lives in North America. Southern copperheads are mostly tan or pink. They have brown bands running around their bodies. Each band is in the shape of an hourglass. Northern copperheads are a brownish gray or a reddish tan color, with dark brown bands. All these colors help to **camouflage** the snakes. They hide in fallen leaves to escape from **predators** and to surprise their **prey**.

The pattern and color of this broad-banded copperhead in Texas helps it to hide among leaves and branches in a forest.

COLD-BLOODED COPPERHEADS

Copperheads are reptiles. Reptiles have backbones and are covered with a skin of dry **scales**. They are also cold-blooded. This means that their body **temperatures** change with the temperature of their surroundings. They warm up by lying in the sun or cool down by seeking the shade. Humans are warm-blooded. Their bodies keep an even temperature no matter how hot or cold it is around them. Snakes cannot keep themselves warm during the winter, so they **hibernate**. Copperheads spend the winter in **dens**. Some share these dens with timber rattlesnakes. When the weather gets warmer, they come out of their dens.

This copperhead peers out from its resting place. Many copperheads live on rocky hillsides and have underground dens.

SNAKEBITE
THE SCIENTIFIC NAME
FOR THE AMERICAN
COPPERHEAD IS
*AGKISTRODON
CONTORTRIX.*

RANGE OF COPPERHEADS

COPPERHEAD HOMES

Five kinds of copperheads live in North America. They are the northern, southern, broad-banded, Osage, and trans-Pecos copperheads. Copperheads are the most common poisonous snakes living in the eastern half of North America. Their homes range from southwestern Massachusetts west to southeastern Nebraska, and then south to Florida. Copperheads also live in parts of Texas and Mexico. Copperheads like to live under logs and in woodpiles. They also like to make their homes on rocky hillsides or near streams, ponds, or swamps. Some copperheads like to live on rocks above canyon riverbeds.

Northern copperheads, such as this one, have dark brown bands that help to camouflage them while they hunt in fields.

A SNAKE WITH CATLIKE EYES

Most copperheads measure between 22 and 36 inches (56–91 cm) long, although one measured 53 inches (135 cm). They are often mistaken for other snakes that have similar colors, such as harmless eastern milk snakes and northern water snakes. One way to tell these snakes apart is by looking at their eyes. Most harmless snakes have round **pupils**. This is because they do most of their hunting during the day. A copperhead's pupils look like upright slits, much like a cat's pupils. Copperheads usually hunt during the day in the spring and the fall. In the summer, they hunt at night to avoid the sun's heat.

All copperheads, such as this southern copperhead in South Carolina, have catlike pupils. If you are close enough to see a copperhead's pupils, you are too close to a dangerous snake!

SNAKEBITE
A COPPERHEAD USES ITS NOSE AND ITS FORKED TONGUE TO SMELL AND TASTE THE AIR.

SNAKEBITE
SCIENTISTS CALL THE PIT VIPER FAMILY VIPERIDAE.

PIT VIPERS

Copperheads are part of a family of snakes called pit vipers. Pit vipers have a pair of pits, or holes, on their faces. The pits are **sensitive** to heat. When a warm-blooded animal such as a bird or a mouse is nearby, a copperhead's pits can sense the animal's exact location. Copperheads are good hunters at night because of their pits.

A copperhead has long, movable **fangs**. When its mouth is closed, the sharp, hollow fangs are folded inside along the top of its mouth. As a copperhead opens its mouth, the fangs swing forward. As the snake strikes, **venom** shoots through the fangs into the prey.

Top: A pit on this northern copperhead can easily be seen. It is the hole near the snake's eye. Bottom: This trans-Pecos copperhead in Texas prepares to strike with its fangs.

13

COPPERHEAD VENOM

Copperheads use venom to kill their prey and to protect themselves from predators. The venom comes from special **sacs** located behind the fangs. Special body parts called venom **glands** produce the venom. Venom is a mixture of poisonous **chemicals**. Each chemical has a job to do when a copperhead bites its prey. One chemical makes the animal bleed inside its body and another slows the animal's breathing. Each pit viper has a special mixture of chemicals.

Copperheads usually try to escape or hide if they see people. If they do bite someone, it is because they feel that they are in danger. Their bites can cause much pain and illness, but they rarely kill people.

Top: This southern copperhead swallows a whole mouse headfirst, as do all snakes. Bottom: The fangs of this southern copperhead helped to kill and to hold a mouse for swallowing.

MATING

Copperheads **mate** during the spring or the early fall. The peak time for mating is from April to May. Sometimes the male snakes fight with each other over who gets to partner with the female copperheads. The two male snakes curl their bodies together and rear up. They do not try to bite each other, but instead they try to push each other's head to the ground. The larger, stronger male copperhead usually wins. Then that male might rub his chin on the ground when he approaches the female. If the female wants to mate with the male, she will whip her tail back and forth. Then the copperheads will mate. From 3 to 9 hours later, the male slithers away.

This female northern copperhead gives birth to live babies that grew inside her body in soft eggs. Males can be two years old when they first mate, but females are usually three years old.

BABY COPPERHEADS

After the males and females mate, they produce babies that grow inside the female in soft eggs. Baby copperheads stay inside the mother's body for about 110 days. Usually in August or early October, a mother copperhead gives birth to fully developed live young. This means that the babies hatch within her at birth or right after she pushes the soft eggs out of her body. A female copperhead can have from 1 to 14 babies at one time. This group of babies is called a brood. Copperheads are born with a yellow or greenish yellow tail, which they use to trick prey. As the prey nears, the snake attacks it.

This young Osage copperhead has a yellowish tail tip that looks like a caterpillar or a worm. Prey may try to capture the tail for a meal but instead the prey will be the snake's meal!

SNAKEBITE
A YOUNG COPPERHEAD'S YELLOW TAIL WILL BECOME GRAY WHEN THE SNAKE IS ABOUT ONE OR TWO YEARS OLD.

SNAKEBITE
SNAKES DO NOT HAVE EYELIDS. THEY HAVE SEE-THROUGH SCALES THAT PROTECT THEIR EYES.

GLOSSARY

antivenin (an-tih-VEH-nun) A medicine used to treat snakebites.

camouflage (KA-muh-flaj) To hide by using a color and a pattern that matches one's surroundings.

cancer (KAN-ser) A sickness in which cells multiply out of control and do not work properly.

chemicals (KEH-mih-kulz) Matter that can be mixed with other matter to cause changes.

dens (DENZ) Wild animals' homes.

fangs (FANGZ) Sharp, hollow or grooved teeth that inject venom.

glands (GLANDZ) Organs or parts of the body that produce an element to help with a bodily function.

hibernate (HY-bur-nayt) To spend the winter in a sleeplike state, with heart rate and breathing rate slowed down.

mate (MAYT) To join together to make babies.

molting (MOHLT-ing) Shedding hair, feathers, shells, horns, or skin.

predators (PREH-duh-terz) Animals that kill other animals for food.

prey (PRAY) An animal that is hunted by another animal for food.

pupils (PYOO-pulz) The openings in the eyes that change size to let the right amount of light into the eyes.

sacs (SAKS) Pouchlike parts in a plant or an animal.

scales (SKAYLZ) The thin, dry pieces of skin that form the outer covering of snakes. Scales are usually made from a matter called keratin.

sensitive (SEN-sih-tiv) Able to see or feel small differences.

temperatures (TEM-pruh-cherz) The heat in living bodies.

venom (VEH-num) A poison passed by one animal into another through a bite or a sting. Venom helps snakes to catch and breakdown their prey as food.

INDEX

WEB SITES

Due to the changing nature of Internet links, PowerKids Press has developed an online list of Web sites related to the subject of this book. This site is updated regularly. Please use this link to access the list:
www.powerkidslinks.com/rwls/copperhe/